D1456983

The Flaming Lemming

written and illustrated by Matt Szychowski

Deep within the woods running alongside the outskirts of
Rainy Daisy Valley lived a little mammal called a lemming. Legend and whisper
spoke of one of the great Echidna Sages blessing this lemming with a special ability.

Those in the village who believed the legends told tales of a lemming that can shoot flames right out of the palm of his hand! And because of this, he was known as the "Flaming Lemming".

One day, the town troublemakers, a chain of
bobolinks known as the Jezappers, had a terrible idea.
"If the legends are true, we can use the lemming's powers to get whatever we want!"

And so they ventured deep into the forest.
Suddenly, a blue flame sparkled far off in the trees.

The Jezappers wandered toward it until they saw with their own eyes the lemming who can shoot fire. Approaching such a creature whilst awake would be unwise, so they waited until night and the lemming went to sleep.

The Jezappers pulled out a potion that they stole from
the town sorcerer. It was a very powerful potion. A few drops of
this potion in someone's eyes would make their sight go away forever.

Living in the woods all alone the lemming was naïve and innocent. So when he woke up, he believed the lie that the Jezappers told about an evil wizard who had put a spell on him. They said that to get his sight back he had to battle the wizard, and that they would help him do this.

So into town they went. Under orders from the Jezappers,
thinking that he was fighting the evil wizard, the Flaming Lemming shot
flames out to scare the workers at the food bank. All of the Jezappers got free food.

Their next stop was the local prison. The Jezappers ordered the
Flaming Lemming to shoot fire at the constable who ran for his life. The
Jezappers chuckled as they broke every one of their bobolink friends out of prison.

From there the Jezappers went into the neighborhood to steal furniture. The parents of a very tiny and babbling little girl finally stood up and refused to give up their sofa. The Flaming Lemming shot fire at her brave parents and their pants caught on fire.

As her parents ran around trying to extinguish their pants, the babbling little girl
heard a far off noise. Something like the small rumblings of an earthquake happened.
And she was one of the few who saw what emerged from the ground in that moment.

One of the mighty Echidna Sages appeared before
the lemming. It was the Echidna Sage of Healing. It laid its
great paw over the lemming's eyes, and the lemming's sight was restored.

The first thing the lemming saw upon regaining
his eyesight was the Echidna Sage. As it faded away,
the lemming noticed the family in peril right before his eyes.

He began to realize that this was his doing.
In the corner he saw the Jezappers snickering as they hauled
the sofa out from the house. Everything began to make sense to him.

Before the Jezappers knew what was going on,
they were running as fast as they could right into prison.

Despite the damage being by his own hand, the people of
Rainy Daisy Valley were extremely grateful to the lemming for catching
the Jezappers. He stayed in the village for a while to help repair the damage he had done.

Then he went back into the woods where he came from.

Very few ever saw him again.
But some say that he was able to walk away from all of the
damage that he had done and went on to live a very happy life.